W9-ANP-617

NO SEW,
NO PROBLEM

No-Sew
POUCHES, TOTE BAGS,
AND OTHER ON-THE-GO PROJECTS

by Samantha Chagollan

CAPSTONE PRESS
a capstone imprint

Snap Books are published by Capstone Press,
1710 Roe Crest Drive, North Mankato, Minnesota 56003
www.mycapstone.com

Library of Congress Cataloging-in-Publication Data
Title: No-sew pouches, tote bags, and other on-the-go projects / by Samantha
   Chagollan.
Description: North Mankato, Minnesota : Capstone Press, 2019. | Series: Snap
   books. No sew, no problem | Audience: Ages 9-14.
Identifiers: LCCN 2018011000 (print) | LCCN 2018015972 (ebook) |
   ISBN 9781543525618 (ebook PDF) |
   ISBN 9781543525533 (library binding)
Subjects: LCSH: Textile crafts–Juvenile literature. | Bags–Juvenile
   literature.
Classification: LCC TT699 (ebook) | LCC TT699 .C475 2018 (print) | DDC
   745.5–dc23
LC record available at https://lccn.loc.gov/2018011000

Editorial Credits
Abby Colich, editor; Kayla Rossow, designer; Jo Miller, photo researcher;
Laura Manthe, production specialist

Image Credits
All photographs by Capstone Studio: Karon Dubke; Craft Product Producers: All done by
Jennifer Reeb

Design Elements: Capstone and Shutterstock

Printed in the United States of America.
PA021

Table of Contents

Crafts for a Life on the Go

You're a busy person! Sports practices, music lessons, and after-school clubs constantly keep you on the go. Whether you're traveling just across town or across the country, you have essentials you need to take with you. Sometimes it's difficult to find just the right travel accessories to meet your needs. So why not make your own? These simple projects don't even require a needle and thread.

Getting Started

Maybe you're a pro at crafting or you're just picking up the hobby. Either way, you'll need a few things for your no-sew projects. Visit your local craft or fabric store for glues and adhesives.

Safety

Safety is important when you are crafting. Always be sure there is an adult nearby to help when you are using an iron, hot glue gun, or other appliance that produces heat. Also have an adult help when using craft knives.

Go, Go Glue

When buying fabric glue, look for permanent fabric adhesive that you can wash once it's dry. Heavy-duty glues are perfect for projects that involve vinyl or heavy fabrics. A glue gun can be the best tool in your craft box! The glue in your gun might not stick to all materials, though, so test it first.

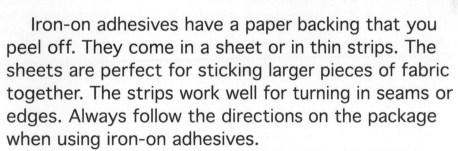

Adhesives

Iron-on adhesives have a paper backing that you peel off. They come in a sheet or in thin strips. The sheets are perfect for sticking larger pieces of fabric together. The strips work well for turning in seams or edges. Always follow the directions on the package when using iron-on adhesives.

Peel and stick adhesives require no iron. These adhesives come on rolls. They are great for sticking small pieces together or embellishments onto fabric.

❧ Travel Tag ❧

Does your bag stand out in a crowd of other bags? Many suitcases and duffel bags look the same. If you're traveling with others or checking your bag at the airport, it can be difficult to find which one belongs to you. This simple tag with brightly colored fabrics and ribbon will add a unique identifying touch to your luggage.

What You'll Need

- 2 pieces of cotton patterned fabric, 3.5 x 5.5 inches (8.9 x 14 cm)
- white cotton fabric, 3.5 x 5.5 inches (8.9 x 14 cm)
- iron and ironing board
- 2 pieces of iron-on adhesive, 3.5 x 5.5 inches (8.9 x 14 cm) each

- business card (for template)
- pencil
- fabric scissors
- fine-tipped permanent or fabric marker
- hole punch
- fabric ribbon, 8 inches (20.3 cm) long

What You'll Do

1. With an adult's help, iron all the fabric pieces to be sure they are flat with no wrinkles.

2. Place a patterned fabric piece facedown on your ironing surface and line up a piece of adhesive on top with the paper side up. Iron for two seconds on medium heat to seal.

3. Peel off the paper on the adhesive and place the white piece of fabric on top, being careful to line up the edges as closely as possible. Iron again to seal.

4. Turn the other piece of patterned fabric facedown. Place the business card in the middle and trace around it with a pencil. Carefully cut out the inner rectangle from the center.

5. Place the fabric over the paper side of the second piece of adhesive. Trace along the edges of the inside rectangle. Carefully cut out the inner rectangle on the adhesive. Repeat steps 2 and 3 to adhere the outer rectangles.

step 5

6. Using fabric scissors, trim the edges of your tag. The fabric adhesive should keep it from fraying, but if your edges become ragged, you can add a line of glue around the edge with a glue gun and add some ribbon trim.

step 8

7. Use a fine-tip permanent or fabric marker to write your name, address, and phone number on the white fabric showing through the window.

8. Punch a hole at the center of the top of the tag. Hold both ends of the ribbon in one hand and thread them through the hole. Then pull the loop back over the ends to secure it on the tag. Now use the ends to tie a secure knot around your luggage handle. Bon voyage!

Tip

To make it extra personalized, add iron-on letters of your initials on the other side.

Perfect Pouch

From earrings and rings to hair ties and barrettes, this drawstring pouch is the perfect place to store small things when you're on the go. The tiny inside pockets are great for your smaller items.

What You'll Need

- cardboard circle, 2.5 inches (6.4 cm) in diameter
- cotton fabric, 4 x 4 inches (10.2 x 10.2 cm)
- fabric glue
- cotton fabric circle, 5.5 inches (14 cm) in diameter
- suede fabric circle, 9 inches (22.9 cm) in diameter

- stick-on fabric adhesive strip, 4 inches (10.2 cm) long
- chalk
- scissors
- 18-inch (45.7-cm) ribbon or cord
- decorative beads or charms

step 1

step 3

What You'll Do

1. Lay the cardboard circle on the back side of the 4- x 4-inch (7.6- x 7.6-cm) piece of fabric. With fabric glue, tack down each corner of the square toward the middle cardboard circle. Then go back around and glue down all four corners again, so your circle is covered in fabric.

2. Place the 5.5-inch (14-cm) fabric circle facedown. Fold down a small bit of the outer edge all the way around and secure with fabric glue to create a hem. This will ensure the edges won't fray on the inside pockets of your pouch. Let dry completely.

3. Turn it over and make an X from end to end with fabric glue. As if you were slicing a pie, add another X of fabric glue so that you have made 8 "slices."

4. Lay the suede circle facedown. Carefully center the smaller fabric circle over it, glue side down, and gently press it into place. Let dry completely.

5. Cut the fabric adhesive strip into thirds. Place the strips on the bottom of the fabric-covered cardboard circle, evenly spaced. Remove the paper backing, center it on top of the other two circles, and press firmly to stick it together.

6. Use the chalk to mark 14 evenly spaced dashes around the suede circle, about 0.5 inch (1.3 cm) in from the edge. Carefully fold the fabric at those spots and make a small snip at each mark.

7. String the cord through the holes, and add some beads or charms to the ends. Tie off the ends and add a bit of glue to secure them in place. Let dry completely.

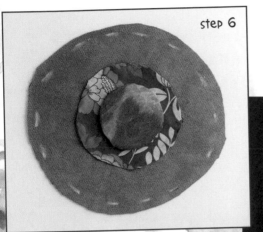

step 6

Tip

Use jar lids or plates and trace with chalk to make fabric circles. The measurements should be close, but don't have to be exact. You can also use a protractor.

Cosmetic Case

Shampoo, check! Toothpaste, check! Soap, check!
Do you need something to store all your toiletries
in when you travel? This simple zippered pack can
keep all your essentials in one pretty place!

What You'll Need

- iron and ironing board
- 2 pieces of canvas fabric, 9 x 16 inches (22.9 x 40.6 cm) and 7.5 x 5 inches (19.1 x 12.7 cm)
- zipper, 7 inches (17.8 cm) long
- craft or fabric glue
- heavy cardboard, 3.25 x 5.25 inches (8.3 x 13.3 cm)
- clothespins or binder clips

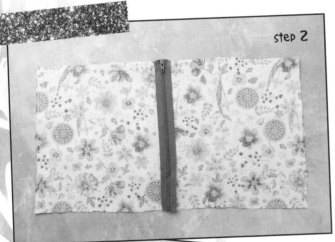

step 2

step 3

What You'll Do

1. With an adult's help, iron out any wrinkles in the fabric. Starting with the larger piece of fabric, fold the short edges in about 0.5 inch (1.3 cm) and iron the creases.

2. Lay the fabric facedown on your work surface. Place the zipper in the middle.

3. Line the edges of the zipper with fabric glue and stick to the outside edges of the folded fabric. Let dry completely.

4. Open up the zipper and turn the pouch wrong-side out. Use a thin line of glue along the outer edges of the open sides to seal the pouch. Let dry completely.

5. Meanwhile, cut a small triangle out of each corner of the smaller piece of fabric. This will be the bottom of your pouch. Turn the fabric facedown and center the cardboard piece on top.

6. Add glue to the edges of the cardboard and fold the fabric over it. Let dry completely. Use clothespins or binder clips to hold the fabric in place until the glue is dry.

7. Once the pouch from step 4 is dry, turn it right-side out again. Tuck in the ends of the zipper and glue in place with a dab of fabric glue. Add clothespins or binder clips to keep it in place until dry.

8. From the outside, push in the bottom two corners about 1 inch (2.5 cm), then open up the pouch and glue these flaps into place inside. Glue the covered cardboard to the bottom of the pouch.

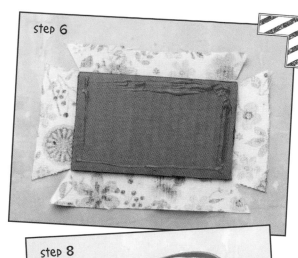

step 6

step 8

Cross-Body Carryall

Whether you're going shopping, taking a day trip, or headed to the beach, this bag is perfect for every occasion. You can even roll it up and stash it in your suitcase when you're traveling. The jersey fabric makes it light and super comfy to carry!

What You'll Need

- king-sized jersey knit pillowcase
- lint roller
- measuring tape
- chalk
- scissors
- thick piece of cardboard, about the size of the pillowcase
- heat transfer foil
- iron and ironing board

What You'll Do

1. Lay the pillowcase flat on your workspace with the opening at the top. Use a lint roller on the pillowcase to be sure you're starting with a smooth surface. Measure up 15 inches (38.1 cm) from the bottom and make a mark on each side with chalk. This is how "tall" your bag will be. Then measure across the top of the pillowcase to find the middle. Make a mark about 1.5 inches (3.8 cm) in each direction from the center.

2. Draw a curved line up from one side mark to the closest 1.5-inch mark on top. Repeat on the other side. Cut along the curved lines through both layers of the pillowcase to create the strap of your bag. Tie the two ends together at the top in a knot.

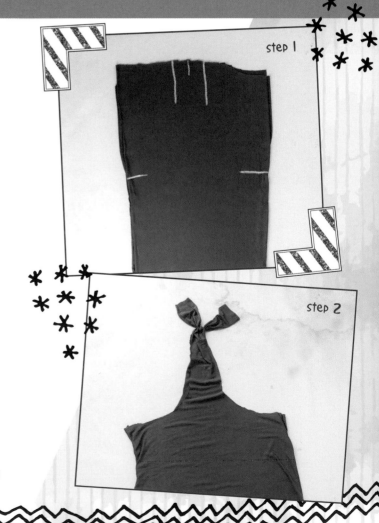

step 1

step 2

3. Place the piece of cardboard in between the two sides so the foil adhesive won't bleed through the fabric.

4. Cut out a design from the heat transfer foil. Follow the package instructions to adhere to the fabric.

5. To add the inside pocket, trim one of the pieces you cut off to about 7 x 5 inches (17.8 x 12.7 cm). Repeat step 4 to add a design to the pocket.

6. Add fabric glue to the inside of three edges of the pocket. Glue near the top center of one side of the inside of the bag. Let dry completely.

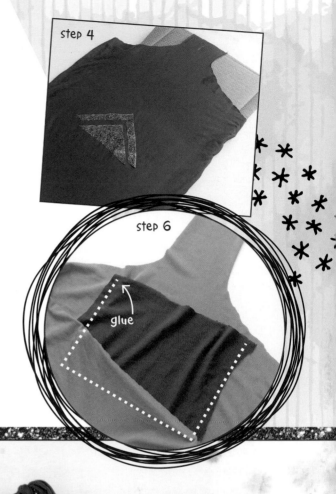

step 4

step 6

glue

Dreamy Mask

Sometimes it's not easy falling asleep in a new place,
but this sleep mask can help you get all your z's.
Whether it's bedtime or you're just taking a quick nap, a
sleep mask helps block out the light. Write SHHH,
NAP TIME, or another sleep-related phrase on your mask.

What You'll Need

- scissors
- 2 pieces of dark fabric (cotton or satin), about 9 x 5 inches (22.9 x 12.7 cm) each
- pencil
- watercolor pencil
- fabric paint marker
- iron-on sparkles
- iron and ironing board
- 12-inch (30.5-cm) strip of elastic
- fabric glue
- clothespins or binder clips
- stuffing

What You'll Do

1. Cut one piece of fabric into the shape of an eye mask. Make sure it's long enough to keep out the light. Start by making it larger and trim as needed until you get the right size. Hold it up to your face to be sure it fits. Once you get the right size, place over the other piece of fabric and trace. Cut out so that you have two identical pieces.

2. Place one of the mask pieces faceup on your work surface. Use a watercolor pencil to sketch out your letters. Make sure they are straight and even.

3. Use a fabric paint marker to go over your lines. If any are still showing when you're done, just use a wet cotton swab to "erase" them.

4. Following package directions, have an adult help iron on the sparkles to adhere them to your mask. Let cool completely.

5. Measure the elastic around your head to make sure it fits. Trim if needed. Lay the other mask piece facedown on your work surface. Add a spot of fabric glue at each side, right and left, and attach the elastic. Use clothespins or bind clips to hold in place. Let dry completely.

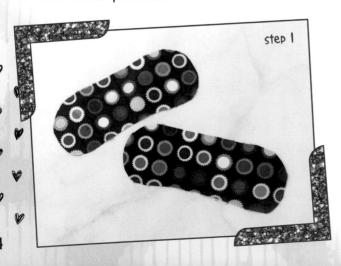

STEP 1

6. Add a bit of stuffing on top of the mask piece. Then draw a thin line of fabric glue around the outside edge all the way around the mask piece.

step 6

7. Take the front of your mask (the piece with the design on it) and line it up carefully on top. Start at one end and work your way around the mask, pressing down firmly as you go.

8. Clamp around the edges with clothespins or binder clips to make sure the pieces don't slide. Let dry completely. The fabric glue should prevent the edges from fraying, but you can always go back with small scissors and trim any small frays or rough edges.

Sleepy Owl Mask

How about a cozy critter mask instead? For a hoot, make a sweet sleepy owl mask. Just cut two circles of light fabric and use fabric paint to draw in the eyelashes. Glue them to the mask, then add the beak and side feathers with fabric paint. Allow everything to dry completely before finishing your mask with elastic and stuffing.

Wash It or Wear It

Ever get your dirty laundry mixed up with your clean stuff in your suitcase? Never again with this little travel laundry bag! Need it for something else instead? It works great for swimsuits or shoes. Use a heavier fabric for shoe bags. Try a utility or waterproof fabric for swimwear. What do you plan to use the bag for? Use the letter stencils to spell it out.

What You'll Need

- muslin or cotton fabric, 24 x 13 inches (61 x 33 cm)
- iron and ironing board
- ribbon or cord, 36 inches (91.4 cm) long
- iron-on fabric adhesive strips
- fabric glue
- cardboard
- letter stencils
- washi tape
- fabric or acrylic paint
- paintbrush or foam brush

What You'll Do

1. Lay the piece of fabric facedown on your workspace, with the long side at the top. Fold both short sides and the bottom long side in 0.5 inch (1.3 cm). With an adult's help, iron the folds to create creases.

2. Fold the top edge in 0.5 inch (1.3 cm). Then fold down another 0.5 inch (1.3 cm) and crease. This will create a space for the ribbon to keep your bag closed.

3. Lay the ribbon inside the fold. Measure and cut enough iron-on adhesive to go along the inside of the first folded flap of fabric. With an adult's help, follow the package directions to iron it into place.

4. Knot each end of the ribbon or cord to be sure it doesn't pull through the bag. For extra security, use two pieces of ribbon or cord and knot them together.

step 3

5. Turn the fabric over and fold it in half so the outer sides are facing each other. Add a strip of iron-on adhesive to the bottom seam, and iron it in place.

6. Turn the bag right-side out, and seal the side seam with more iron-on adhesive. You may need to add a spot of fabric glue at the corners to keep everything in place.

7. Place a piece of cardboard inside your bag so that the paint doesn't seep through to the other side. Tape your stencils into place with washi tape.

8. Paint (or dab) the letters onto your bag. Let dry completely before using.

step 5

Tip

No stencils? No problem! Use rubber stamps and fabric paint or fiber-friendly ink to stamp your label on your bag. Or design something on a computer and print it out on iron-on fabric transfer paper.

Monogram Cup Cozy

Give your warm beverage a personalized touch with a monogrammed cup cozy. It's fancier than the plain old cardboard version! It's also less wasteful since you can reuse it again and again. They make great gifts for friends too.

What You'll Need

- cardboard cup sleeve from a takeout cup
- scissors
- flannel or burlap fabric, about 10 x 6 inches (25.4 x 15.2 cm)
- fabric glue
- light-colored cotton fabric, about 3 x 3 inches (7.6 x 7.6 cm)
- pencil
- iron-on monogram letter
- crystals, buttons, ribbon, or other embellishments
- 1 small adhesive hook and loop fastener dot

What You'll Do

1. Cut or separate the cardboard sleeve so it is flat. Lay your fabric facedown. Place the flat cardboard sleeve on top. Fold the fabric around it and glue it in place. Cut off any extra fabric. Let dry completely.

2. Trace a small circle (you can use a roll of tape as a template) onto the light-colored fabric. Make sure the entire circle will fit on your cozy.

3. With an adult's help, follow the package directions to iron a monogram letter onto fabric circle. Let cool. Glue circle to middle of cozy. Let dry completely.

step 1

step 5

4. Embellish with glue-on or iron-on crystals. If you use a heavier fabric, like burlap, glue ribbon around the edges with fabric glue so it doesn't fray.

5. Center the hook and loop fastener dot at one end of the outside of the cozy and attach. Wrap the cozy around a cup to find where to attach the hook and loop fastener dot on the inside of the other end.

Earbud Grabbers

Do you get annoyed when you go to pull your earbuds out and they are a tangled mess? These little keepers will make sure your wires don't get crossed.

What You'll Need

- vinyl fabric, 5 x 5 inches (12.7 x 12.7 cm)
- small jar lid to use as a template, about 3 inches (7.6 cm) in diameter
- chalk
- scissors
- permanent markers or acrylic paint
- 1 adhesive hook and loop fastener dot

What You'll Do

1. Turn the vinyl facedown and trace a small circle on it, about 3 inches (7.6 cm) in diameter.

2. Cut it out carefully. Make sure the edges are smooth.

3. Flip it over so it's faceup. Choose a design you like and use permanent markers or acrylic paint to create it.

4. Once your design is dry, cut the adhesive dot in half. Take one half and adhere it to the top edge of each side of your vinyl. (Save the other half of the circle for another earbud grabber!)

5. Wrap your earbuds around your hand and then tuck them inside the earbud grabber. No more tangles!

step 1

step 4

Tip

You can find some great stuff in the remnants section of your fabric store! Look for vinyl or upholstery fabrics there.

Semicircles for Friends

These adorable earbud grabbers make great gifts! Personalize with names, initials, or phrases. You can also make these with any design that works on a half circle! Try making donuts, tacos, pizza, citrus slices, rainbows, and more! Play around and practice on some scrap paper first to find the one you like the best.

Clever Clutch

This little clutch is perfect for your tablet or a small notebook. Make it a larger size if you need it to hold a larger tablet or even a book! Paper doilies work great to create the design, but you can also find some inexpensive fabric versions at a dollar or craft store. Try out different patterns on paper first to find a design you like. This bold pattern is so much fun to make, you're going to want to try it on everything!

What You'll Need

- light-colored faux leather fabric, 10 x 15 inches (25.4 x 38.1 cm)
- ruler
- chalk or pencil
- scissors
- lace or paper doilies
- spray-on fabric paint
- contrasting piece faux leather fabric, 5.25 x 10.25 inches (13.3 x 26 cm)
- fabric glue
- 1 adhesive hook and loop fastener dot

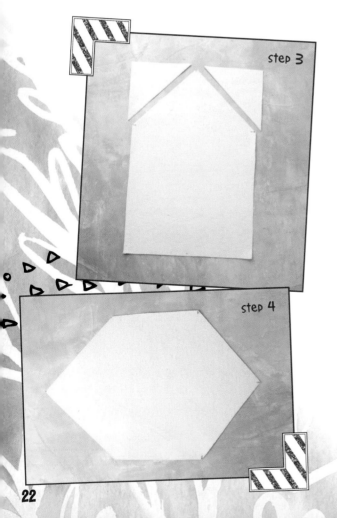

step 3

step 4

What You'll Do

1. Lay the light-colored piece of fabric facedown on your workspace, with the short sides at the top and bottom. Mark a dot with chalk at the top center of the piece halfway across. Make another mark at the halfway mark along the bottom.

2. Measure 5 inches (12.7 cm) down from the top of each long side of the fabric, and make a mark there too.

3. Using the ruler, draw a straight line from one side mark to the top center mark. Repeat for the other side. Cut along the lines to make a triangle at the top.

4. Measure up 4 inches (10.2 cm) from the bottom, and make a mark on each side. Again, draw two straight lines from the center bottom mark to the marks on the two sides. Cut along the lines to create a triangle at the bottom.

5. Flip the fabric over and place the doilies on top of it. You may need to trim them or cut them in half to get the design you want.

6. Spray the fabric paint over the doilies, creating a delicate pattern. Keep the doilies in place and allow the paint to dry overnight.

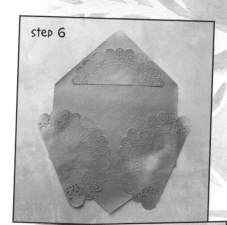
step 6

7. Flip the painted piece of fabric over so that it's facedown. Take the contrasting piece of fabric and lay it facedown. Line the two short edges and one long edge of the backside with glue. Make sure the unglued long end is at the top. Center it carefully just below the top triangle. Glue in place. Let dry completely.

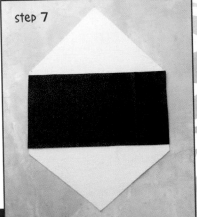
step 7

8. Fold up the bottom triangle and glue it onto the contrasting fabric. Center and attach the hook and loop fastener dot near the top of the upper triangle. Fold down and make sure the other end of the hook and loop fastener dot is centered directly underneath and attach.

Tip

If you don't have faux leather, you can use vinyl. Thicker vinyl can make it difficult for the fabric glue to do its job. Use a couple of heavy books to hold the pieces in place overnight while they dry.

Cord Keeper

Keep all the cords for your technology in one place with this easy roll-up. Never dig through your bag for your charger again.

What You'll Need

- vinyl or faux leather, 7 x 18 inches (17.8 x 45.7 cm)
- dinner plate
- pencil
- metal ruler
- scissors or craft knife
- 1 adhesive hook and loop fastener dot
- oil-based paint pens

What You'll Do

1. Place the vinyl piece facedown on your work surface with the shorter end at the top. Use the dinner plate to trace a curved edge along the top and then cut out.

2. Measure 3.5 inches (8.9 cm) in from one of the longer sides. Draw a light pencil line through this point from top to bottom.

3. Measure about 0.25 inch (0.6 cm) from both sides of that line. Draw two more light lines from top to bottom through those points.

4. Use the scissors or craft knife to cut three or four 2.5-inch- (6.4-cm-) long slits along both outer lines that you drew. This is what will keep your cords in place.

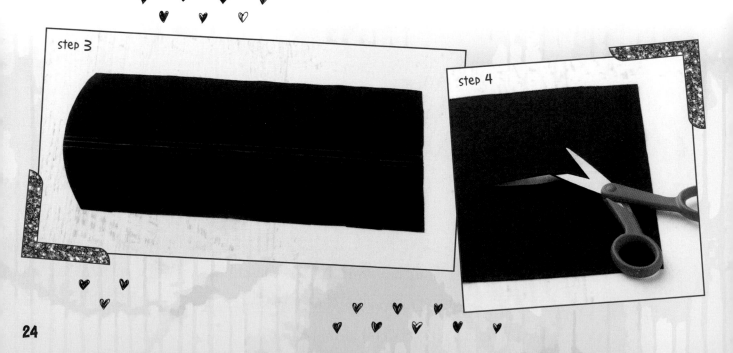

step 3

step 4

5. Center the hook and loop fastener dot along the inside of the top curved edge and adhere. Try placing some cords inside and rolling it up to see where the other piece of the hook and loop fastener should go. Adhere the other side of the dot.

6. Decorate the top and the sides with oil-based paint pens. Allow it to dry completely.

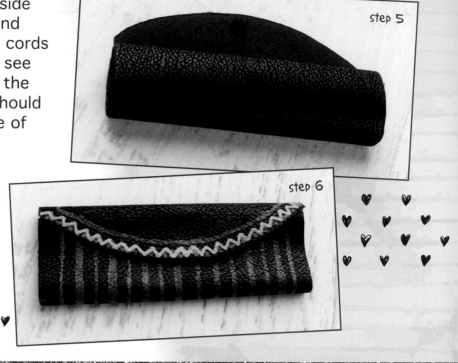

step 5

step 6

Shady Case

You're headed outside on a bright, sunny day. Don't forget
your sunglasses! Keep them in this colorful case and
they'll be easy to spot in your bag! The metallic fabric
paint looks like metal studs. If you want another look,
try adding a fun fabric trim such as fringe or pom-poms.

What You'll Need

- small dish or plate, about 8 inches (20.3 cm) in diameter
- chalk
- patterned fabric, about 10 x 10 inches (25.4 x 25.4 cm)
- sheet of craft felt in a contrasting color
- iron-on adhesive sheet, at least 10 x 10 inches (25.4 x 25.4 cm)
- scissors
- iron and ironing board
- hot glue gun and glue sticks
- clamps
- metallic fabric paint

step 4

What You'll Do

1. Turn the plate facedown and trace it onto the fabric, the felt, and the adhesive. Cut out each circle.

2. With the back side of the patterned fabric facing up, place the adhesive on top (paper side up). With an adult's help, iron in place. Let cool completely.

3. Peel off the paper. Lay the felt circle on top. Following the package directions, iron the felt in place. Let cool completely. If needed, carefully trim the edges of your circle to even them out.

4. Fold the circle in half. Use the edge of the plate to trace a curved line at the top, like someone has taken a bite out of the top of the fabric. Cut along the line through both layers of the circle.

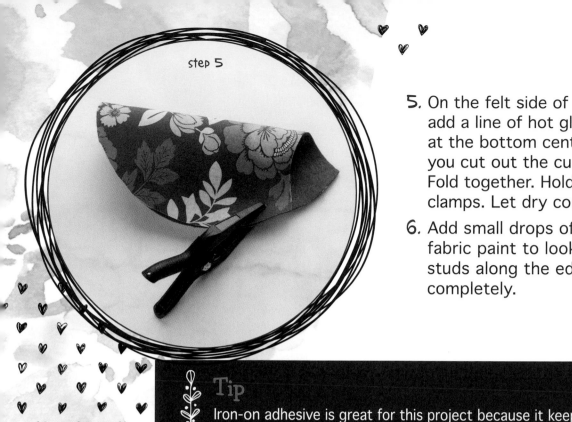

step 5

5. On the felt side of the circle, add a line of hot glue, starting at the bottom center to where you cut out the curved piece. Fold together. Hold in place with clamps. Let dry completely.

6. Add small drops of metallic fabric paint to look like metal studs along the edge. Let dry completely.

Tip

Iron-on adhesive is great for this project because it keeps the two fabrics fairly flat. But if you're having trouble getting the felt to stick to the fabric, you can also use a strong fabric glue.

Hold That Charge

Time to charge your phone again? Just find an outlet and let this little fabric holder do the rest. It keeps your phone off the floor while it charges and keeps the cords from getting tangled too. You may need to change the measurements to make sure your phone fits inside.

What You'll Need

- cotton fabric, 12 x 4.5 inches (30.5 x 11.4 cm)
- fabric glue
- contrasting cotton fabric, about 5 x 5 inches (12.7 x 12.7 cm)
- scissors
- 3 strips of jersey fabric, about 10 x 0.5 inches (25.4 x 1.3 cm)
- 4 inches (10.2 cm) of peel and stick fabric adhesive tape

What You'll Do

1. Place the large piece of cotton facedown on your work surface. Fold in the short sides about 0.5 inch (1.3 cm) and glue down.

2. Flip the piece faceup. Add glue along the edges to the bottom half of the two long sides. Fold the top half down to glue in place. Let dry completely.

3. Turn the bag right-side out. Cut a small slit near the top edge of each side of the bag, just under the top seam.

step 3

4. Braid the three long strips of the jersey fabric for the strap. Tie knots at each end to hold the braid in place.

5. Thread each end of the braid through the inside of the bag, securing it with a knot on the outside. Double knot both sides.

6. Trim out a pattern from the contrasting fabric, about 2.5 by 2.5 inches (6.4 by 6.4 cm). Peel and stick fabric adhesive on the back. Press it firmly in place. Peel the other side and attach to the center front of the bag.

step 4

Wrist Wallet

Going on a quick trip down the block? Or need something to carry just a few items? This little wrist wallet is great for carrying a little bit of cash, your ID, and even some lip gloss. It's the perfect accessory for when you're on the go.

What You'll Need

- stretchy fabric, such as jersey, 12 x 9 inches (30.5 x 22.9 cm)
- zipper, 4 inches (10.2 cm) long
- fabric glue
- clothespins or binder clips
- 3 small adhesive hook and loop fastener dots
- acrylic or fabric paint

What You'll Do

1. Lay the piece of fabric facedown.

2. Apply fabric glue to the edges of the zipper. Fold one of the shorter edges of the fabric under about 0.5 inch (1.3 cm) and glue it to one edge of the zipper. Repeat with the other short end of fabric and the other zipper edge. Use clothespins or binder clips to hold in place. Let dry completely.

3. Unzip and turn inside out. Glue the edges of the long sides together to create seams. Use clothespins or binder clips to hold in place. Let dry completely.

4. Turn right-side out and glue the top seams together around the zipper. Add clothespins or blinder clips again and allow to dry completely before continuing.

step 2

step 4

5. Evenly space the dots along one end of the front of the wallet and adhere. Wrap the wallet around your wrist with the zipper on top. Note where the other ends of the hook and loop fastener dots should go to keep the wallet in place. Adhere the other sides of the hook and loop fastener dots to the backside of the wallet. Don't make the hook and loop fastener dots too close or else the wallet will be too tight around your wrist. But don't make it so loose that it could fall off. Remember that once you put some stuff inside, it will stretch out a bit.

6. Decorate the front of your wallet with acrylic or fabric paint. Let dry completely before using.

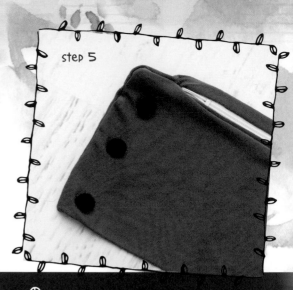

step 5

Tip

Jersey is a nice fabric to use for this project because it has a little stretch to it. But you could make this out of denim or another fun fabric instead!

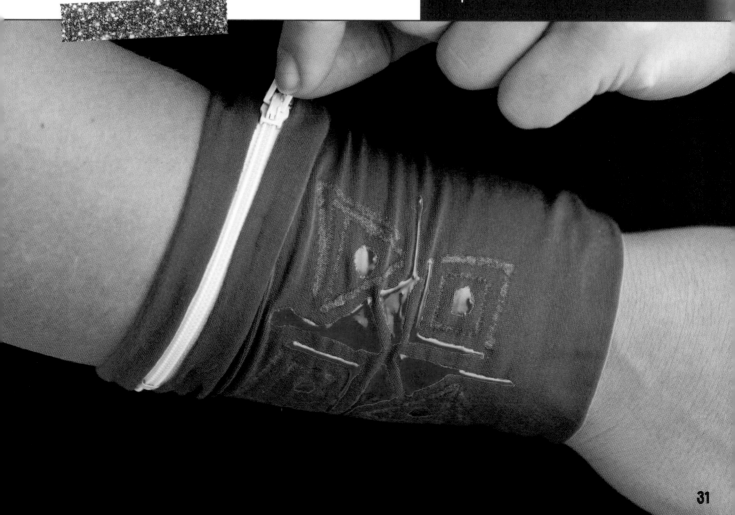

Read More

Blum, Nicole, and Catherine Newman. *Stitch Camp: 18 Crafty Projects for Kids and Tweens*. North Adams, Mass.: Storey Publishing, 2017.

Fields, Stella. *Accessory Projects for a Lazy Crafternoon*. Lazy Crafternoon. North Mankato, Minn.: Capstone Press, 2016.

Johnston, Ashley. *No-Sew Love: 50 Fun Projects to Make Without a Needle and Thread*. Philadelphia: Running Press, 2014.

Internet Sites

Use FactHound to find Internet sites related to this book.

Visit *www.facthound.com*

Just type in 9781543525533 and go.